Kids CAN!

28-Day Family Devotional

Upholding the Biblical Value of Work

HENDRICKSON PUBLISHERS

ROSE KiDZ

www.hendricksonrose.com

Kid's Can!

Upholding the Biblical Value of Work

Copyright © 2019 Theology of Work Project

RoseKidz® is an imprint of
Rose Publishing, LLC
P.O. Box 3473
Peabody, Massachusetts 01961–3473 USA
www.hendricksonrose.com

Written by Leah Archibald for the Theology of Work Project
Interior and cover design by Drew McCall

ISBN: 978-1-68307-218-8
RoseKidz reorder #K72188
RELIGION/Christian Life/Devotional

Printed in United States of America
Printed March 2019

Table of Contents

Introduction

From the moment they wake up in the morning, kids do important work.

- They might start the day with chores that help maintain their home.

- They may troubleshoot a fight with a brother or a sister.

Learning to work within a family is a type of work all its own.

At school, kids work on:

- School subjects like writing and math

- Making friends and keeping them

- Pleasing their teachers

- Figuring out how to deal with peers, authorities, and their own limitations

> God cares a lot about kids and the work they do.

All these lessons travel with kids into the adult world.

Meanwhile, kids are starting to wonder about economics. They want to know how money works and how they can get some of it for themselves. They might be asking adults, "What can I do for money?" It's time to start giving them answers.

God cares a lot about kids and the work they do. The Bible teaches that all work is important and that all people have work to do.

That doesn't mean a kid's work is easy. The Bible explains why work is tough and what to do in the face of challenges. In fact, the Bible has many practical tips on work. These lessons can give kids the best chance they have at being successful, happy, and fulfilled.

Each devotion in this book includes:

- A story about a kid facing a real-life problem

- Biblical wisdom for dealing with similar problems

- Questions for discussion

- Prayers

- Suggestions to help you take these lessons into daily family life

It might take some work carving out the time to interact with Scripture every day as a family, but it's worth the effort. Through twenty eight days of focusing on the Bible and work, you will build the foundation kids need to work well at home, at school, and in the economy.

Part 1

Kids
Work at
Home

Day 1

Everyone Has Work to Do

Genesis 2:15,19

The Lord God placed the man in the Garden of Eden to tend and watch over it. . . . So the Lord God formed from the ground all the wild animals and all the birds of the sky. He brought them to the man to see what he would call them, and the man chose a name for each one.

A Kid's Story

Sean woke up to his little sister shouting, "NO!"

Through the doorway of his bedroom, Sean could see Riley stomping her foot in the hallway wearing only a diaper. Sean's stepfather was standing above her, holding out a pink dress. Riley was hugging a pair of fuzzy pajamas to her chest.

"NO!" Riley screamed.
"I do it myself!"

"Sweetie, you can't wear fleece pajamas when it's eighty-five degrees outside."

"I do it myself!" Riley yelled back.

"Look, let me help you put on this dress. I have to go soon. I'm working today."

Riley screamed, "NO! *I'm* working today!"

The Bible Connects with Life

A toddler can be loud while she works out what her job is. When a kid slows down the work of the house, parents can get loud and frustrated, too. In all this noise, you might forget that work is a good thing. But everyone—toddlers, kids, and grownups—is made to work. Everyone wants meaningful work to do. God designed us this way.

When God made the first person, God gave him a job. Genesis 2:15 says that God put Adam in the garden "to tend and watch over it." God also gave Adam the job of naming all the animals. God created them, and Adam named them. They worked as partners.

A home is a place for partnership, too. Imagine your family is a team. Each one of you has different skills, likes, and dislikes. God put your family together for a reason.

A home is a place for partnership, too. Imagine your family is a team.

Parents and Kids Try This Together

Name one thing you do at home that makes you feel proud of yourself. It could be a skill like cooking a tasty meal or putting together a cool outfit. Or, it could be something you do for the sake of the household, like raking leaves or washing the dishes. Whatever job makes you feel proud, say, "God created me to

_____.

When I _____,
I'm helping my family team, and I'm partnering with God!"

Prayer

God, thank you for making me the way I am. Help me see the importance of the work I do at home today. Help me see the work of those around me today. In Jesus' name, amen.

It Hurts When No One Notices Your Work

Matthew 25:34-40

"Come, you who are blessed by my Father, inherit the Kingdom prepared for you from the creation of the world. For I was hungry, and you fed me. I was thirsty, and you gave me a drink. I was a stranger, and you invited me into your home. I was naked, and you gave me clothing. I was sick, and you cared for me. I was in prison, and you visited me."

Then these righteous ones will reply, "Lord, when did we ever see you hungry and feed you? Or thirsty and give you something to drink? Or a stranger and show you hospitality? Or naked and give you clothing? When did we ever see you sick or in prison and visit you?"

And the King will say, "I tell you the truth, when you did it to one of the least of these my brothers and sisters, you were doing it to me!"

A Kid's Story

Sean pulled up a seat at the breakfast table.

"Pancake!" Riley screamed from her highchair. Mom placed a pancake on Riley's tray.

"Do you have your baseball permission form?" Mom asked, passing Sean a plate.

"I guess it's in my backpack." Sean answered.

His mother sighed. "I'll grab it. We're running late."

As his mom walked out of the kitchen, Riley threw her pancake to the ground. "Not like that!" she complained.

Sean looked at Riley. "What's wrong? You want syrup on it?"

Riley nodded. Sean served her a new pancake, this time with syrup. She scooped it up quickly. Most of the syrup missed her mouth and poured over her face, hands, and stomach. "Oh well," thought Sean, "At least she's not wearing clothes."

Their mother came back into the kitchen and gasped. "What on Earth is all over your sister?"

"Um, maple syrup?" Sean answered.

"Honestly, I expect a little more from you," his mother snapped. "I work hard around here. I need you to start helping out."

Sean got angry. "I help all the time!" he growled, gesturing at his sister. "Why don't you notice the work I do?"

The Bible Connects with Life

- If your work goes unnoticed, do you get angry?

- Do you wish you got points for all the work you do—like living in a video game and hearing a "ka-ching" sound every time you did something good?

Sadly, our work is not always immediately rewarded. It can feel frustrating when no one pays attention to the good things we're doing.

In Matthew 25, Jesus says that God is always paying attention. God cares about the work we do, especially the work no one else notices. Jesus says that God will give away the Kingdom to people who do good work that no one sees. When you notice the hard work of the people around you, you're doing an important job for God.

God cares about the work we do, especially the work no one else notices.

16

Parents and Kids Try This Together

Imagine the work of your house is a video game. Every time you do something that should earn points, yell, "KA-CHING!" Try this one day while you're doing chores as a family. Then, talk to each other about how it felt.

LET'S PLAY!

Prayer

God, thank you for always seeing the work I do. Help me notice the work other people do in my home. In Jesus' name, amen.

Day 3

Work and Play Together as a Family

Luke 10:38–42

As Jesus and the disciples continued on their way to Jerusalem, they came to a certain village where a woman named Martha welcomed him into her home. Her sister, Mary, sat at the Lord's feet, listening to what he taught. But Martha was distracted by the big dinner she was preparing. She came to Jesus and said, "Lord, doesn't it seem unfair to you that my sister just sits here while I do all the work? Tell her to come and help me."

But the Lord said to her, "My dear Martha, you are worried and upset over all these details! There is only one thing worth being concerned about. Mary has discovered it, and it will not be taken away from her."

18

A Kid's Story

When Sean came home from baseball, he found his stepdad under the kitchen sink.

"Come play catch with me!" Sean said.

"Hold on. I'm fixing a leak."

Sean waited.

"Hand me the hex wrench."

"Is that the circle one?"

"It's the—never mind, I've got it."

Sean waited some more. "How long will it take?" he asked.

"I can't play right now, Sean, but I'll come out when I'm done working."

Sean pounded his fist into his glove. "You're always working!" he said, and stormed out.

At dinner that night, Sean's mom said, "It's time for a family meeting. We haven't been working well together. How can we do better?"

Sean thought. "We could point out the work that other people are doing," he said. "Like, thanks for fixing the sink, dad. Can I help you on your next job?"

"Sure," said his stepdad. "And we should also make time to hang out and relax. Let's put something fun on the calendar for every work project we finish."

"Those are great ideas," Mom said. "What do you think, Riley?"

"Cupcakes!" Riley exclaimed.

Sean and his stepdad laughed. Their mom frowned and said, "Cupcakes make a mess."

"That's OK," said Sean. "If you help us make them, we'll do the cleanup."

His mother smiled. "Now that's working together!"

19

The Bible Connects with Life

Each person has a list of things to do. When your list is different from someone else's, there can be trouble. You might get annoyed when someone interrupts your work. Or you might get impatient with someone who's working when you need them.

Annoyance and impatience make teamwork hard.

Jesus helped two sisters see this. Martha was cooking dinner while Mary talked with Jesus. "Tell her to help me!" Martha complained (see Luke 10:40). But Jesus didn't do that. Martha felt her work was the most important, she was annoyed with her sister, and she interrupted impatiently. Family members can't work as a team that way.

If your family has trouble working together, talk about it. Make time for relaxing together, too.

Annoyance and impatience make teamwork hard.

Parents and Kids Try This Together

Think of one household task to do together as a family. Think of one fun thing to do together. Schedule time to do them both!

Prayer

God, thank you for the
people in my family.
Help us be unworried and
attentive to each other. Bless
us in our work and play.
In Jesus' name, amen.

Day 4

Whose Job Is It to Clean Up?

1 Corinthians 12:12–13,18–22,27

The human body has many parts, but the many parts make up one whole body. So it is with the body of Christ. . . . God has put each part just where he wants it. How strange a body would be if it had only one part! Yes, there are many parts, but only one body. The eye can never say to the hand, "I don't need you."

The head can't say to the feet, "I don't need you." In fact, some parts of the body that seem weakest and least important are actually the most necessary. . . . All of you together are Christ's body, and each of you is a part of it.

A Kid's Story

Alaysha was sitting on the couch with a big bowl of snacks in front of her watching a show.

Her peace was interrupted when her mom came in with the vacuum. "Juan and his parents are coming over at five o'clock," she said.

"Yay! What are we having for dinner?" Alaysha asked.

"Spicy chicken, grilled the way you like it. You'll need to clean and vacuum your room before they get here."

Alaysha groaned. "Do I have to?"

"Yes."

"How come I have to do all the boring chores? Why can't I grill the chicken and you vacuum?"

"Because I asked you to vacuum your room. And because you don't know how to use the grill. Besides, I am vacuuming. I'm vacuuming this room now and you're vacumming your room when I'm done." Mom turned on the vacuum.

"Hey! I can't hear my show!"

"In that case, you can take your snack into the kitchen. While you're there, clear your stuff off the table."

"I never get to do anything fun, just clean this, clean that!" Alaysha yelled over the vacuum. "Why do I get stuck with all the boring jobs?"

23

The Bible Connects with Life

Does this interaction sound familiar to you? The only thing that's less fun than doing chores is trying to get someone else to do them. Yet chores are the first step in getting to the fun things you do in your home. If you want a nice space to play, then you need to clean it. If you want delicious things to eat, then someone needs to cook.

You might feel like you get stuck with the worst chores because you're younger than other people in your family or because you don't know how to make elaborate meals. But your family still needs you. There's something you can do to help. Everyone has a different part in your family, just like your body has many different parts. If you want to do a cartwheel, all the parts of your body need to work together. If you want things to work right at your house, all the parts of your family have to work together, too.

> Chores are the first step in getting to the fun things you do in your home.

Parents and Kids Try This Together

In the space below, name three things that someone else in your family does for you.

Prayer

God, help my family work together as different parts of one body. In Jesus' name, amen.

Day 5

Stop the Fuss over Chores

2 Thessalonians 3:10–13

Even while we were with you, we gave you this command: "Those unwilling to work will not get to eat." Yet we hear that some of you are living idle lives, refusing to work and meddling in other people's business. We command such people and urge them in the name of the Lord Jesus Christ to settle down and work to earn their own living. As for the rest of you, dear brothers and sisters, never get tired of doing good.

A Kid's Story

Alaysha sat on the floor in her room playing with the toys she was supposed to be putting away. Her mother appeared in the doorway.

"I asked you to clean this up," her mother exclaimed. "Why is there still stuff everywhere?"

Alaysha threw her body onto the floor with great drama. "It's too much! I can't do it myself! You need to help me!"

"I'm making dinner," her mother replied, exasperated.

"Then you should pay me for cleaning this all by myself," Alaysha said. "What will you pay me?"

Her mother's eyes narrowed. After a long pause, she looked at Alaysha and replied, "Dinner."

The Bible Connects with Life

In your house, do you feel like a hired helper? Do you begrudge the people in your family for not rewarding you for your work?

You're right that work entitles you to a reward. Proverbs 14:23 says that all hard work brings a profit. But when it comes to work in your home, you can't profit at someone else's expense. Each person's work benefits everyone else in the family. And everyone else's work benefits you. That's why you don't get paid to do chores. You wouldn't want someone to pay you to clean your room if it meant you had to pay someone else to make dinner!

In the Bible, the leaders who traveled around teaching about Jesus made sure they always did their share of work, instead of expecting other people to serve them. They encouraged others to do the same thing. Do your part without making a big deal about it. You can trust that you will get everything you need in return.

"Work brings profit, but mere talk leads to poverty."
Proverbs 14:23

Parents and Kids Try This Together

A non-financial reward for work could be:

- Relaxing in a clean home

- Enjoying a nice meal as a family

- Feeling pride at doing a job well

- Feeling the joy of being helpful

As a family, take turns thinking about the chores you do, and come up with at least one non-financial reward you get from doing each chore.

Prayer

Thank you, God, for everything that comes from you, both the things I work for and the gifts you give freely. In Jesus' name, amen.

Day 6

Chores Bring Us Together

Ecclesiastes 4:9–12

Two people are better off than one, for they can help each other succeed. If one person falls, the other can reach out and help. But someone who falls alone is in real trouble. Likewise, two people lying close together can keep each other warm. But how can one be warm alone? A person standing alone can be attacked and defeated, but two can stand back-to-back and conquer. Three are even better, for a triple-braided cord is not easily broken.

A Kid's Story

"We fought a lot about chores today," Alaysha's mother said. "Let's write down a plan to do better."

Alaysha groaned. "Is this another chore chart?"

"No, it's more like a web," her mother said, taking a piece of paper and writing the name of a family member in each corner.

"Here are the people who live in this house. And here are tomorrow's chores," she said, making a list down the center of the page. The list included cook breakfast, fold laundry, and other chores. "We could think of these as things we have to do, but I see them as things we do because we love each other."

Mom drew a line from her name to cook breakfast. "When I make breakfast, I'm helping you start your day with energy." She continued the line to Alaysha's name. "That makes you happy. And it shows I love you."

She drew a line from Alaysha's name to fold laundry to Mom's name. "When you put away the clothes, I know that everything is ready when I need it. That makes me feel loved."

She drew more lines connecting the members of her family to their chores and to the people who benefit from them. "We've each got many different ways to show that we love each other."

"OK." Alaysha said, "I get it. Can I keep the picture? I want to remember how to love you next time."

The Bible Connects with Life

Chores show the people you live with that you care about them. You may not like doing them, but you'll like the results that come from your work: happy parents, proud kids, a clean place to live, and a family who likes being together.

The writer of Ecclesiastes encouraged people to work together because "a triple-braided cord is not easily broken" (Ecclesiastes 4:12). This image applies to chores directly: Three people can clean a house better so the cleanliness isn't soon broken. But it's true of your family, too. When you work together, your relationships aren't easily broken. You value each other more and fight less. Those are results worth working for.

Chores show the people you live with that you care about them.

Parents and Kids Try This Together

On a blank sheet of paper, draw your own family chore web and post it somewhere you can all see.

Prayer

God, help me love my family through my work today. In Jesus' name, amen.

When Brothers and Sisters Fight

Genesis 13:8-9

Finally Abram said to Lot, "Let's not allow this conflict to come between us or our herdsmen. After all, we are close relatives! The whole countryside is open to you. Take your choice of any section of the land you want, and we will separate. If you want the land to the left, then I'll take the land on the right. If you prefer the land on the right, then I'll go to the left."

A Kid's Story

Esther spread a sheet of newspaper onto the kitchen table. On top of it she placed three tubes of paint and a wooden jewelry box. She dipped a tiny paint brush into a glass of water. "Hmm, which color first?" she thought. "I'll start with a big red heart."

"Can I paint, too?" her little sister, Hannah, asked.

"No," Esther said through pursed lips. "You're not careful with paint."

"Come on. Let me help," Hannah said. She leaned on the table.

"Get off, you'll mess everything up!" Esther whined.

Hannah crossed her arms. "Fine," she said coldly. "That's my paint brush."

"No, it's not!" Esther protested.

"It's mine!" Hannah screamed, grabbing the brush out of Esther's hand. Esther reached for it, but Hannah hid it behind her back. Esther leaped at Hannah, tackling her to the ground. Their mom walked in just at that moment.

"Esther, go to your room."

"It wasn't my fault!" Esther protested.

"I don't care whose fault it is," their mother said. "If you're fighting, you need to separate. Esther, upstairs, now."

The Bible Connects with Life

Brothers and sisters. They always want to tag along. But they don't play what you want to play. And there's not enough stuff for both of you. No wonder siblings fight!

One of the Bible's heroes, Abraham, had a younger family member who gave him trouble. Lot tagged along with Abraham. That was OK most of the time. But Abraham and Lot had to separate when they started fighting over stuff. So Abraham let Lot choose where he wanted to be, and then Abraham went in the other direction. To Abraham, it was more important to end the fight than to get exactly what he wanted.

Fights over stuff can get ugly quickly. When a brother or sister shouts, "mine!" it's good to get a little distance and time apart.

When a brother or sister shouts, "mine!" it's good to get a little distance and time apart.

36

Parents and Kids Try This Together

Next time you're getting angry with your sibling, take five and five: five steps backward and five deep breaths. If you still feel angry, take five more. Wait until then to say or do anything.

Prayer

God, help me remember you when I'm feeling angry. Help me and my siblings work together. I trust that you give me everything I need. In Jesus' name, amen.

What's Fair between Siblings

Genesis 13: 11–16

Lot chose for himself the whole Jordan Valley to the east of them. He went there with his flocks and servants and parted company with his uncle Abram. So Abram settled in the land of Canaan, and Lot moved his tents to a place near Sodom and settled among the cities of the plain. But the people of this area were extremely wicked and constantly sinned against the LORD.

After Lot had gone, the LORD said to Abram, "Look as far as you can see in every direction—north and south, east and west. I am giving all this land, as far as you can see, to you and your descendants as a permanent possession. And I will give you so many descendants that, like the dust of the earth, they cannot be counted!"

A Kid's Story

Esther sat on the edge of her bed, fuming. Her sister always got her into trouble. It wasn't fair!

Esther's mom appeared in the doorway. "Are you feeling calmer now?" she asked.

"It wasn't my fault," Esther complained. "I was just trying to paint, and Hannah stole my brush! She always does that. Then you sent me to my room. You always take her side!"

Esther's mother sighed. "You think I always take your sister's side?"

"Of course you do!" Esther said. "She's the baby. You like her best!"

Esther's mom sat down next to her. "Oh, honey, I don't like either of you best. I love both of you completely. Sure, I treat you differently. But that's because you're different ages. You need different things. Your younger sister needs more hand-holding. You need practice working things out on your own. I expect different behavior from you because you're older. But my love isn't uneven. I love you all the way, all the time. Both of you."

The Bible Connects with Life

What's fair? Does fair mean that you get what you want? That everyone gets the same thing? That everyone gets what they need?

Rather than cause a fight, Abraham decided to give Lot what he wanted so it would work out for both of them. In the end, it did work out for Abraham. God gave Abraham everything he needed—and more.

Sometimes you get so upset over something you want that you forget what you need. Fighting over what's fair often leads to nobody getting anything they want or need.

Fighting over what's fair often leads to nobody getting anything they want or need.

Parents and Kids Try This Together

Try to go a whole day without saying the word *fair*. When you want to say something isn't fair, say something else like, "I'm mad that I'm not getting what I want," or, "I need something right now—what do you need?"

Prayer

God, thank you for loving me completely. I love you, too. Please give my siblings what they need. Help me to trust that you'll take care of me, too. In Jesus' name, amen.

Pull Together When It Counts

Genesis 14:14-16

When Abram heard that his nephew Lot had been captured, he mobilized the 318 trained men who had been born into his household. Then he pursued Kedorlaomer's army until he caught up with them at Dan. There he divided his men and attacked during the night. Kedorlaomer's army fled, but Abram chased them as far as Hobah, north of Damascus. Abram recovered all the goods that had been taken, and he brought back his nephew Lot with his possessions and all the women and other captives.

A Kid's Story

Esther's mother suggested they go downstairs for snacks when they heard a sharp scream.

"It's Hannah!" Esther said, racing out the door with her mother close behind.

Hannah stood in the kitchen, glass everywhere. Across the front of her soccer jersey was a rapidly spreading red spot. It wasn't blood. It was paint! Hannah had leaned on the table and toppled everything onto herself. The glass was in pieces on the floor.

"Help!" Hannah said.

"Don't move," said her mother. "I'll get the vacuum."

Esther was more afraid for Hannah's soccer uniform. "Toss me your shirt," she said. "I can keep it from staining if I wash it quickly."

Hannah nodded gratefully. Esther brought the shirt to the sink. The cold water ran red over Esther's hands. Then it turned pink, and after a few minutes it was clear. Esther held up the shirt for Hannah to see. All that was left of the accident was a faint, pink, blotchy heart.

"I like it even better now!" Hannah said. Then she added, "I'm sorry I wasted your paint."

Esther took a deep breath. "I forgive you," she said. "But I don't know how to finish my jewelry box now."

"Maybe I could hold your jewelry?" Hannah offered.

Esther laughed. "No way!"

The Bible Connects with Life

Even if we fight with siblings, we come together in a crisis. You should be able to count on your brother or sister when you're in trouble. And if your brother or sister needs help, you should pause any fights to help them.

When Abraham heard that Lot was in trouble, he stopped everything he was doing to help. Abraham used everything he had to save Lot from danger.

It's natural to see a brother or sister as your rival. But a sibling can also be your closest ally. As often as you're fighting with them, make sure you're fighting for them. You'll want them to fight for you when it counts.

If your brother or sister needs help, you should pause any fights to help them.

Parents and Kids Try This Together

Think of something that members of your family fight about. Pretend that each member is the ruler of a neighboring country. Draft a treaty of alliance between the rulers with terms of peace.

Prayer

God, bring peace to my family. Help us stand up for each other. You can do anything, God. In Jesus' name, amen.

Part 2

Kids Work at School

Hope at School

Matthew 5:3

God blesses those who are poor and realize their need for him, for the Kingdom of Heaven is theirs.

A Kid's Story

Lucas sat at the breakfast table, folding his math homework into a tiny football. When the paper triangle was tight enough to tuck in the edge, he balanced the paper football on the table and flicked it toward the wall.

"Lucas," his mother said sternly, "do you have your school stuff packed? Where's your math homework?"

Lucas pointed to the paper football on the floor. His mother grabbed the paper and unfolded it.

"Lucas, you didn't finish half the problems! Quit goofing around. You've got to get this done."

"I can't," Lucas said.

"Not with that attitude!"

"No, I really can't do it. I can't do the problems. I'm bad at math."

Lucas's mother paused and looked at him. "You really think that way?"

He nodded.

"Lucas, you're not bad if you can't do a few problems."

"I'm not?"

"No! You just need some help!"

"OK, fine," Lucas said. "Help me then!"

The Bible Connects with Life

Have you ever felt bad at school? If you can't learn something, it has nothing to do with being good or bad. It just means you need some help. God put people together to help each other. If you're struggling at school, there's probably a teacher who can help you. You have to ask for help to get it.

God blesses people who are poor and realize their need for him. If you're poor at math or anything else at school, God promises his blessings when you admit you need him. God works through the people around you, so ask them for help. You might feel bad at first, but Jesus says you'll end up feeling blessed.

If you can't learn something, it has nothing to do with being good or bad. It just means you need some help.

Parents and Kids Try This Together

Name one thing you're "poor" at doing. Make up a super-un-hero who is the worst at this, and tell a story. For example, Math Disaster Man couldn't count down from ten, so his rocket launched backward. See who can tell the funniest story. Talk about who each super-un-hero could have asked for help.

Prayer

God, help me when I feel I'm poor at things. Give me willingness to learn new things and your power to do it. In Jesus' name, amen.

Day 11

When School Makes You Sad

Luke 6:21

God blesses you who weep now, for in due time you will laugh.

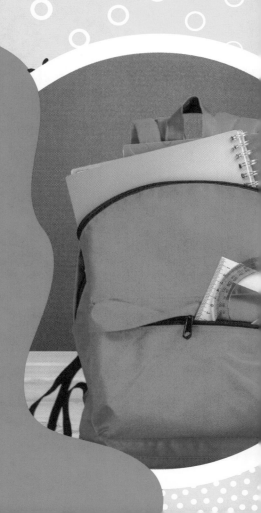

A Kid's Story

"Do you have more unfinished homework?" Lucas's mom asked, picking up his backpack and pulling out a crumpled piece of paper.

Lucas watched his mother's face turn red. Oh no, he thought. She's found the math quiz.

"What is this?" she asked angrily.

"A quiz. I told you I was no good at math."

"Why did you leave it crumpled in your bag?"

"Maybe I didn't want you to get mad," Lucas said. He looked down at the floor. "I feel bad enough about it already."

His mother flopped into a chair. "Well I *am* mad!" she said. She was quiet for a minute. "How do you feel about it, Lucas?"

"I don't know. Sad I guess," he said.

"Well," said his mom, "that's good. Sad gives us a place to start. If you didn't care at all, I'd have to throw up my hands and give up!" She laughed. Lucas laughed a little bit, too.

"But if you're sad," she continued, "at least it means you want to change. Let's think together of what we can do. I trust you'll follow through with whatever we decide because I know you want to fix it."

The Bible Connects with Life

Everyone fails sometimes—even parents. It's normal to feel sad when you fail.

If you feel sad about something you did or didn't do, you don't have to hide it. The best way to stop being sad is to talk to someone about it. Tell someone you trust about the problem. You can ask for forgiveness if you've done something wrong, and you can ask for help. Together you can work to solve the problem. God says you're blessed when you're sad out loud because soon you'll be laughing (see Luke 6:21).

If you feel sad about something you did or didn't do, you don't have to hide it. The best way to stop being sad is to talk to someone about it.

Parents and Kids Try This Together

On scraps of paper write down five things that make you feel bad about school or about work. Put the papers in a bowl. Pick one hardship and describe it dramatically, using three different emotions. First sad, then mad, and finally happy.

For example:

- Write, "Math is too hard." Act overdramatically sad and cry, "Math tests are a tragedy!"

- Next, beat your chest like the Hulk screaming, "Argh! Math homework! Must destroy!"

- Finally, act out being happy. Jump around and say, "More math problems? Goodie, I loooove math!"

Who can be silliest?

Prayer

God, please turn my sadness to joy. I trust you, God. In Jesus' name, amen.

Day 12

Ask a Teacher for Help

Matthew 5:5

God blesses those who are humble, for they will inherit the whole earth.

A Kid's Story

In the car on the way to school, Lucas and his mom talked about what he might say to his teacher. "Do you want to come in with me?" Lucas asked.

"No. I think you can be brave," His mom answered.

Lucas's math teacher was alone in the classroom. He smiled when Lucas walked in.

"Lucas! I wasn't expecting you. What's up?"

Lucas took a deep breath. "I came to talk about my quiz," he said. "And about the stuff we're learning now. I'm not . . . um . . . I think I need some help."

"I'm glad you came in," the teacher said. "I know lots of ways to help. Did you try the flashcard method?" Lucas looked at him blankly. "The one we practiced in class last week?"

Lucas shook his head, "I guess I wasn't paying attention. Sorry."

"That's OK," the teacher said, pulling up a chair for Lucas. "You're here now. Let's work on it together."

The Bible Connects with Life

Do you want to walk into your school or into work like you own the place? Like you're powerful? Like you're in control? The Bible has a funny trick for this: Be humble.

Moses, the most powerful leader of ancient Israel, was described in Numbers 12:3 as "very humble—more humble than any other person on earth." Jesus described himself as "humble and gentle at heart" (Matthew 11:28–29). It might seem strange, but you can feel better at school or at work by becoming more humble.

Jesus said that the humble will inherit the earth. That means school, business, even the world can be yours, if you put aside pride and be honest about your strengths and weaknesses. How do you think God wants you to approach your work today?

How do you think God wants you to approach your work today?

58

Parents and Kids Try This Together

Remember your story about a super-un-hero? Now imagine your school is a secret training program for super-un-heroes to discover their powers. You are a hero in training. What superhero teachers would help you? Write down the names of all real teachers, helpers, friends, or family who might be helpful to you. Give them each a superhero identity, like Mathbrainiac or Sidekick Flashcard. Imagine asking them to go on a top-secret mission with you to develop your superpowers.

Prayer

God, you see my struggles.
Help me see the people
around me who can help.
My hope is in you, God.
In Jesus' name, amen.

Day 13

Help When You Don't Like Your Teacher

1 Timothy 2:1–2

I urge you, first of all, to pray for all people. Ask God to help them; intercede on their behalf, and give thanks for them. Pray this way for kings and all who are in authority so that we can live peaceful and quiet lives marked by godliness and dignity.

A Kid's Story

"What's up, Hannah?" her father asked from the driver's seat. "You're usually so excited to go to school and see your friends. Today you're quiet. Is something wrong? Did you and Carlie get in a fight?"

"No," Hannah said. "Nothing's wrong with Carlie or any of my friends. It's my teacher, Ms. Mitchell. I hate her."

"Wow, that's a strong word," her dad said. "You hate your teacher?"

"She's so mean! She's always yelling at me for talking. I hope we have a substitute today."

"I didn't know you were frustrated with your teacher," Her dad paused. "Did you try praying for her?"

Hannah made a snorting sound with her nose. "Praying for her? What would that do?"

"I don't know, it might help her," he replied. "And it would definitely make you feel better."

"Like if I pray for her to be absent?" Hannah asked.

"No," her dad answered. "Pray for her to be healthy! Pray she has everything she needs to do her job well. Thank God for her."

Hannah snorted again. The car pulled up to the curb and she opened the door.

"Hey," her father said, catching her eye. "I'm praying for you and Ms. Mitchell today."

The Bible Connects with Life

A teacher or a boss has a lot of power over your life. If you hate your teacher or your boss, then your life during the day is no fun. The Bible gives us advice for dealing with these troubles. The first tip is to pray for everybody in authority, including bosses and teachers.

First Timothy gives us ways to pray for people in power. Pray that they do their jobs well, and thank God for them. It probably feels hard to thank God for a teacher you don't like. But praying helps you, too. It helps you feel calmer. It reminds you that God is in charge. God can do things you can't do. Plus, prayer helps you think of things to make the situation better.

Pray for everybody in authority, including bosses and teachers.

Parents and Kids Try This Together

Think of three things that make you happy. (Seeing a friend? Eating your favorite food? Hearing a funny joke?) Now, ask God to give each of these to your teacher or boss today.

Prayer

God, bless the authorities in my life with everything they need. I trust you to give me everything I need, too. In Jesus' name, amen.

Don't Fight with a Teacher

Romans 12:21–13:3

Don't let evil conquer you, but conquer evil by doing good. Everyone must submit to governing authorities. For all authority comes from God, and those in positions of authority have been placed there by God. So anyone who rebels against authority is rebelling against what God has instituted, and they will be punished. For the authorities do not strike fear in people who are doing right, but in those who are doing wrong.

A Kid's Story

Hannah felt Carlie grab her hand under the desk and drop in something small. Hannah looked at Ms. Mitchell to make sure her back was turned. Then she peeked. It was an eraser shaped like a strawberry with arms and legs and a smiling face. Hannah giggled.

"It's one of my favorites," Carlie whispered. "But you can have it."

"Carlie! Hannah!" Ms. Mitchell got their attention. "We're talking about the Bill of Rights. Can either of you tell me the First Amendment?"

"Um, the right to remain silent?" Carlie guessed.

"No, that's not it," Ms. Mitchell said.

Carlie looked down at the desk, embarrassed. Hannah thought of the perfect joke to cheer her up.

"She should have called it the Bill of Wrongs!" Hannah exclaimed, a little louder than she had meant to.

Some kids laughed, but others gasped.

"Hannah," Ms. Mitchell said angrily. "Hallway. Now."

The Bible Connects with Life

Correction and punishment are sometimes part of a teacher's job. If you're the one getting corrected or punished, you might feel like you have a right to mock your teacher or not listen to what they say. Sadly, disrespecting a teacher will hurt more than it helps. Disrespect makes it hard for a teacher to respect you. If you want school to improve, you can't "let evil conquer you," as Romans 12:21 puts it. You need to "conquer evil by doing good."

You can turn around teacher trouble by showing respect. Words like sorry, please, and thank you are all signs of respect. So is looking at your teachers when they speak and doing the work you're asked to do. With respectful practices, you and your teacher will start getting along.

If your teacher is actually hurting you or other kids, talk to another authority, such as—a parent, principal, or adult you trust. These authorities can keep you safe. God does not want anyone to hurt you.

Disrespect makes it hard for a teacher to respect you.

Parents and Kids Try This Together

Compete to be the most respectful. How many times can you say sorry, please, or thank you? Keep a secret count and reward the person who did more today.

Prayer

Lord, you have authority over all things. Help me act rightly at school. Protect me from unjust punishment. I trust you, God. In Jesus' name, amen.

Day 15

Help Your Teacher

Proverbs 16:7, 25:21–22

When people's lives please the LORD, even their enemies are at peace with them.... If your enemies are hungry, give them food to eat. If they are thirsty, give them water to drink. You will heap burning coals of shame on their heads, and the LORD will reward you.

A Kid's Story

Hannah stood in the hallway and fumed. She hated her teacher. She thought of all the angry words she'd like to say. Then she sighed. Being angry wasn't going to solve her problem. What could?

With irritation, Hannah remembered her father's suggestion. She didn't have any other ideas, so she started to pray.

"Help me, God. Help me pray for Ms. Mitchell. Please... I don't know... make her a good teacher. Make her students good, too."

Suddenly, Hannah thought about what it might be like to be Ms. Mitchell. Maybe her job wasn't all that easy. Maybe she was frustrated that her students didn't pay attention.

Even though Hannah was still angry, she started to wonder if there was something she could do to help Ms. Mitchell. She prayed some more, and when her teacher came into the hallway, Hannah was ready.

"I'm sorry I was disruptive," she said. "And I have an idea to get kids excited about the lesson. That is, if you'll let me help."

That afternoon, Hannah couldn't stop talking when she got into the car.

"Dad! You'll never believe it! I took over Ms. Mitchell's class by making a game," she said. "The kids competed to memorize the amendments. The winner got a strawberry eraser!"

"And your teacher was happy?" her dad asked.

"She said thank you about a million times. She probably feels terrible for yelling at me. Now she'll have to be nice to me because she wants me to help run the class again next week!"

The Bible Connects with Life

It's a good idea to be helpful to your teacher. This is true whether or not you like your teacher and whether or not you think they're fair. Even if your teacher seems like your enemy, being helpful in the classroom will end up helping you the most. You'll get peace from it. You might even get rewarded.

The book of Proverbs says that people who live in a way that pleases God get rewarded. They get along with everyone—even their enemies. Proverbs 25:22 says helpfulness is the best revenge against someone who is mean to you. It's like pouring burning coals on their head!

Even if your teacher seems like your enemy, being helpful in the classroom will end up helping you the most.

Parents and Kids Try This Together

Play teacher and students. Pretend you're a terrible teacher with good students. Then try being a good teacher with unhelpful students. What about a terrible teacher with terrible students? After each exercise, ask, "What did you need from me? How could I have been helpful?"

Prayer

God, you are the best teacher. I believe you can help me at school today. Thank you, God. In Jesus' name, amen.

Day 16

Make New Friends at School

Philippians 2:3–4

Don't be selfish; don't try to impress others. Be humble, thinking of others as better than yourselves. Don't look out only for your own interests, but take an interest in others, too.

A Kid's Story

José looked across the playground at a group of boys kicking a soccer ball. He wanted to join in, but his feet seemed glued to the spot where he was standing—right outside the door of his new school. How do kids make new friends? José wondered.

The doors opened, and a boy José's age walked onto the playground.

"Hi! You must be new," the boy said. "I'm Martin."

"I'm José," he replied. He couldn't think of anything to say after that.

"What do you like to do, José?" Martin asked.

"MonsterGo!" José gushed. "I have more cards than anyone I know!"

"Never heard of it," said Martin.

"Well, I always win because I have four fire dragons. Once, my cousin played a water serpent against me, but I still beat him."

"Well, later, Monster Kid," Martin said, before turning and running toward the soccer field.

"I was just about to ask what you like to do!" José called after him. But Martin didn't hear.

The Bible Connects with Life

You might think you'd make friends by impressing people, but no one wants to be friends with a bragger. When you talk only about yourself, people think you're vain or selfish. It is better to be humble, as Philippians 2:3–4 suggests. Ask about the other person and what interests them.

Think about a conversation with a friend as a game of trading information. Try to listen more than you talk. Listen actively by looking at their eyes and pointing your body in their direction.

No one wants to be friends with a bragger.

Parents and Kids Try This Together

Practice a trading-information conversation. Pretend you just met and you're trying to get to know each other. Take turns talking, and listen actively. Kids can also get practice making conversation by talking on the phone with other kids.

Prayer

God, help me speak humbly and listen actively. Give me someone new to talk to today. I want to learn from you how to be a friend. In Jesus' name, amen.

Play with Kids You Don't Know

Acts 18:1–3

Paul left Athens and went to Corinth. There he became acquainted with a Jew named Aquila, born in Pontus, who had recently arrived from Italy with his wife, Priscilla... Paul lived and worked with them, for they were tentmakers just as he was.

A Kid's Story

José approached the soccer field. There were several boys passing balls back and forth. A ball rolled toward José. Someone yelled, "Kick it back!"

José didn't move. "Are you going to play a game?" he asked.

"No," the boy answered. "Just messing around."

"You should play a game with teams," José said.

The boy shrugged and ran down the field. He didn't say anything more to José.

How was José supposed to make friends if everybody ran away from him?

José noticed two boys crouching near a soccer goal. There was a snapping turtle inside the goal. Every time a boy got close, the turtle would bite.

"What are you doing?" José asked.

"Trying to move this turtle, but it's mean."

José thought of a way to work with the boys. "Maybe you could pick it up with something, like a stick."

"Or, if we had two sticks, we could pick it up like tongs," a boy answered. "Let's try!"

"I'll help you," José said. "I'm José."

"I'm Carl. I don't like turtles."

"I like frogs," José said.

"My brother had a pet frog," Carl said. "Until my mom found it."

José smiled. Together José and Carl looked for sticks.

The Bible Connects with Life

Working together is a great way to make friends. When you're trying to join in with a new group, first watch what they're doing. Don't criticize or try to change their game. Do what they're doing (as long as it's safe), ask if you can help, and they'll quickly see you as a friend.

Someone in the Bible who often had to make new friends was the Apostle Paul. He moved around a lot, and he made friends by joining in the work that other people were doing. When he moved to Corinth, Paul made friends with Aquila and Priscilla. They worked together making tents. They also worked together teaching other people about Jesus. They became such good friends that when Paul moved away, he wrote about them, saying,

Give my greetings to Priscilla and Aquila, my co-workers in the ministry of Christ Jesus. In fact, they once risked their lives for me. I am thankful to them, and so are all the Gentile churches (Romans 16:3–4).

God gives us many jobs, like taking care of creation and making sure a turtle gets safely out of the way. Lots of God's jobs are so big that no one can do them alone. By working together, people become friends, and friends enjoy working together.

Working together is a great way to make friends.

Parents and Kids Try This Together

Brainstorm places where you can meet people while working together, like a volunteer group or a sports team. Maybe role play meeting someone new at one of them. Then, actually try one new thing this week.

Prayer

God, give me work to do today and friends to do it with. In Jesus' name, amen.

Day 18

How to Keep the Friends You Have

Proverbs 18:24

There are "friends" who destroy each other, but a real friend sticks closer than a brother.

A Kid's Story

The snapping turtle was still sitting in the soccer goal, even though José and his new friends had tried pushing it, poking it, and lifting it between two sticks.

"I know, let's flip it!" Carl said. He put the end of his stick under the turtle and pushed hard. The turtle flipped into the air and landed on Carl's leg.

"Argh! Get it off!" he screamed.

José burst into laughter, "That was dumb!"

"Owwwweeee!" Carl yelled as the turtle bit him. He scowled at José. "Stop laughing, jerk!"

José put his hand over his mouth. Carl stared at him with eyes like lasers.

"I'm sorry," José said. "Are you OK?"

"Yeah." Carl said. He wiped his nose. After a minute he said, "That was pretty cool, right?"

"Totally cool!" said José.

The Bible Connects with Life

Being a friend means caring about what the other person might be feeling. This is called empathy. When you see someone hurt or embarrassed, do you laugh? Or do you show concern and try to help? If your first response isn't that of a real friend as described in Proverbs 18:24, then you can practice your empathy.

If you want to remain friends with others, it's important to stick by them when something goes wrong. Don't make fun of a friend who is hurting. Say sorry, even if it's not your fault. According to Proverbs 18:24, this is what real friends do.

Being a friend means caring about what the other person might be feeling.

Parents and Kids Try This Together

Practice figuring out how people feel. Read the story of the Good Samaritan (Luke 10:30–37) or another book you like. Discuss each of the characters in the story: What does each person feel? What do they want? How do we know it?

Prayer

God, here's a prayer for the friends I haven't met yet. Make them happy. Help me be a good friend to them. In Jesus' name, amen.

Part 3

Kids Work in the Economy

Budg
In

E

Day 19

The Basics about Money

Proverbs 14:23

Work brings profit,
but mere talk
leads to poverty!

A Kid's Story

Sophia burst into the kitchen where her mom was paying bills.

"I need a new bike," she said.

"Hmm," her mom answered.

"My bike is slow, and Jenna just got a new one," Sophia continued.

"It's a lot of money for a new bike," her mom said, frowning at the bill in her hand.

"You make money," Sophia protested. "Isn't money for spending?"

"Hmm," her mother said again. "This seems like a good time to teach you the basics of money."

The Bible Connects with Life

Money isn't a secret code or a magic weapon. It's simply a tool of exchange. Money lets you turn your work into things you want. Before money, people could only barter. If you wanted something you couldn't make, you'd have to find someone who had such an item and who wanted to trade. But that person might not want what you have to trade in. Money lets you sell your work to the people who want it and store up value from your work to spend later.

When a parent gives you money, they had to earn it first. You can spend it in exchange for something someone else made, or you can invest it so that other people work and pay you back more money later. You can also give it away to someone who can't work. Each of these options appears in the Bible. It's important to know what money represents—real-life work.

What's important is knowing what money represents—real-life work.

Parents and Kids Try This Together

Have a conversation about your family rules around money. Where does parents' money come from? How much money are kids allowed to spend without parent's approval? How can kids make their own money? When can kids spend parent's money? Is gift giving limited to birthdays and holidays? What types of purchases do you consider necessary?

Prayer

God, thank you for whatever money I have. Give me the willingness to honor you with all my choices. Show me how to make good decisions about money. In Jesus' name, amen.

Day 20

Know the Limits of Money

Ecclesiastes 5:10

Those who love money will never have enough. How meaningless to think that wealth brings true happiness!

A Kid's Story

"So, you know where money comes from?" Mom asked to see if Sophia was paying attention.

"You have to earn it," Sophia answered. "And if you work more, you'll make more money!"

"That's true," Mom said. "But there's something else you need to know about money. Something that's also always true."

"What's that?" Sophia asked.

Her mom made a grave face. Finally, she said, "Money is always *limited*."

The Bible Connects with Life

Money isn't infinite. It represents real work. You are limited in the type of work you can do and the amount of time you can spend doing it. So your money is limited, too. This is true for everyone, from the poorest person to the richest billionaire. No one has enough money to buy every single thing they want. They might try to make more and more money to keep up with their desires, but there will always be more things to want. You buy something new and then you get bored with it. Money and objects can't keep you happy forever. In the end, there's no amount of money that can buy happiness.

Many places in the Bible, including Ecclesiastes 5:10, say that there's never a perfect dollar amount that feels like enough. These verses encourage you to ask God for fulfillment and put money in its place. God is unlimited, and God is the source of true and lasting happiness. If you see things that way, you can be happy and make wise money decisions.

Many people get wise about money by tracking exactly how much they earn and spend. You can use a budgeting program to do this, or just write down each transaction in a notebook.

> God is unlimited, and God is the source of true and lasting happiness.

Income
Salary
Other

Giving

Saving

Housing
Mortg
Utilit
Insur
Oth

Tra
Ca
In

Parents and Kids Try This Together

Practice tracking the flow of money in and out of your household. For one week, write down every time you get money and every time you spend it or give it away. Write down the date, the amount of money, and what it was for. When the week is up, look back at your list and think about what you learned. If you're learning a lot, you can keep on tracking!

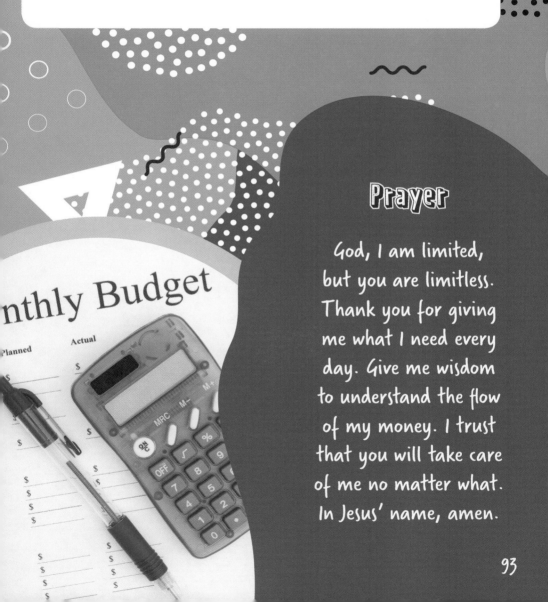

Prayer

God, I am limited, but you are limitless. Thank you for giving me what I need every day. Give me wisdom to understand the flow of my money. I trust that you will take care of me no matter what. In Jesus' name, amen.

Day 21

Make Difficult Money Decisions

Luke 14:27-29

If you do not carry your own cross and follow me, you cannot be my disciple. But don't begin until you count the cost. For who would begin construction of a building without first calculating the cost to see if there is enough money to finish it? Otherwise, you might complete only the foundation before running out of money, and then everyone would laugh at you.

A Kid's Story

"You know, Mom," Sophia said, "I thought when you were a grownup you could just buy whatever you wanted. Now I see you can't spend money without thinking first. To get money, you have to work for it. Or someone else has to work and give it to you."

"Right," Her mom replied. "So, you want to talk about this new bike now?"

"I don't understand! I thought this whole money lecture was your way of saying no new bike. Now you're saying yes?"

Her mother laughed, "I don't want to say yes or no. I want us to practice thinking through decisions together. Let's start by figuring out whether the bike is worth the cost."

The Bible Connects with Life

When you're thinking about a difficult decision, it helps to compare the cost to the benefits. Jesus even suggested people do this before following him. In Luke 14:27–33, Jesus points out that both kings and builders figure out whether they are able to pay the cost before starting projects. Why not do the same for all important decisions?

On one side of a piece of paper, write down all the benefits of a specific decision. On the other side, write down all the costs. It might be a dollar amount, or it might be something other than money. For example, the benefits to buying a new bike might include fitting in with other people, getting more exercise, or feeling safer. The costs to buying a new bike might include spending extra time on housework as payback, missing out on time with friends, or disappointment when you want a new thing later. Writing everything down helps you see the options more clearly.

There is something else to consider—the spiritual costs and benefits of each decision. Giving money away to people in need has huge spiritual benefits. Your faith in God increases, and when you give generously, and you'll find you have less stress about your other money decisions.

> Giving money away to people in need has huge spiritual benefits.

Parents and Kids Try This Together

Make a cost-benefit analysis of a decision you're considering. If you need to choose between different options, make a cost-benefit analysis for each option and then compare them. What did your analysis show you?

Prayer

God, I want to follow you in all my decisions. Thank you for being a worthy guide. In Jesus' name, amen.

Day 22

Get a Job by Working Hard

2 Thessalonians 3:7–10,13

For you know that you ought to imitate us. We were not idle when we were with you. We never accepted food from anyone without paying for it. We worked hard day and night so we would not be a burden to any of you. We certainly had the right to ask you to feed us, but we wanted to give you an example to follow. Even while we were with you, we gave you this command: "Those unwilling to work will not get to eat." As for the rest of you, dear brothers and sisters, never get tired of doing good.

Application for Emp

Please fill out form completely for employment consideration
completed.

Position Applied For:

cial Security No.:

legal

Last Name

City

il Address:

ation:

est school grade

ou have a high school

ber of years of past high

and Location of
tional Institution:

Degree Rec

98

A Kid's Story

"The best thing about third grade at this school," Carlos told his friend Mark, "is you get to apply for principal's helper. The principal's helpers have the coolest job. Instead of going straight to class in the morning, they hang out in the principal's office and make announcements over the loud speakers!"

"Wow," Mark said. "I want that job. How do you get it?"

Carlos looked grave. "You have to write an application and then do an interview with the principal. He wants to see that you're a good worker."

"A good worker? How do you show that?" Mark asked.

"I don't know exactly," Carlos said. "My teacher always says the motto of our school is hard work. Maybe the principal is looking for kids who can prove they work hard?"

The Bible Connects with Life

Bosses want hardworking employees.

The evangelist Paul was an example of a hard worker. He started dozens of churches and wrote a quarter of the New Testament. He could have asked others to support him financially, but Paul continued to work as a tentmaker wherever he traveled. He "worked hard day and night," as he puts it in 2 Thessalonians 3:8, to be a model of how other Christians should work.

You can show you're hardworking by doing more than is asked of you. Instead of just filling out an application for a job, write a letter to the boss saying what goals you'd set for yourself in the position. Think of a story that shows you do more than just show up. Did you bike extra miles at the school bike-a-thon? Did you read twenty books when the summer reading list had ten? Do you consistently fold your laundry instead of throwing it in the drawer? If you can't think of an example of working hard, start now by setting a goal and going for it.

You can show you're hardworking by doing more than is asked of you.

Parents and Kids Try This Together

Next time someone asks you to do something, go the extra mile. If you're asked to set the table for dinner, arrange everything like a restaurant. If you're asked to work in a group at school, see if you can help someone in the group who's behind.

Prayer

God, thank you for the chance to work hard. Help me enjoy all the work I do. In Jesus' name, amen.

Day 23

Get a Job by Being Dependable

Luke 16:10

If you are faithful in little things, you will be faithful in large ones. But if you are dishonest in little things, you won't be honest with greater responsibilities.

Proverbs 31: 15–18,31

She gets up before dawn to prepare breakfast for her household and plan the day's work for her servant girls.

She goes to inspect a field and buys it; with her earnings she plants a vineyard.

She is energetic and strong, a hard worker.

She makes sure her dealings are profitable; her lamp burns late into the night.
Reward her for all she has done. Let her deeds publicly declare her praise.

A Kid's Story

In addition to their applications, Carlos and Mark each wrote a letter telling about a time they had worked especially hard. The principal was impressed and invited them for an interview. Carlos and Mark were nervous.

"What do you think it'll be like? Will he ask hard questions?" Mark questioned Carlos.

"My mom told me not to worry about the questions. She said that, knowing me, there's just one thing I need to worry about," Carlos said.

"What's that?"

Carlos cracked a smile, "Showing up on time."

The Bible Connects with Life

Once a boss can tell you're hardworking, they want to know that you're dependable. Dependability means being reliable, trustworthy, doing what you said you would to do. Small actions demonstrate this—it doesn't need to be big stuff. Something as simple as showing up on time and bringing a pencil to take notes shows that you're dependable. People who see you acting dependable in small ways will trust you with bigger responsibilities. Jesus promised this when he said, "If you are faithful in little things, you will be faithful in large ones."

If you want to show dependability, make sure you have the time and materials to do the thing you've said you'd do. When you're going to school, practice, or an interview, leave early so you have enough time to get there, even if there's a holdup. Before you leave, check to make sure you have everything you'll need. The woman in Proverbs 31 does this. She wakes up early to make sure everyone has what they need for the day. She is energetic in the way she works. At the end of the day, she evaluates whether her work went well. She is an example of dependability.

> Dependability means being reliable, trustworthy, doing what you said you would to do.

Parents and Kids Try This Together

Think of the most dependable person you know. If you can, interview that person. What are their daily work habits? What makes them able to be dependable? If you can't interview them, think about one thing they do that shows dependability. Could you try doing that?

Prayer

God, I have faith that you can do all things. Help me be a person other people can depend on. In Jesus' name, amen.

Day 24

Get a Job by Being Positive

Philippians 1:3-6

Every time I think of you, I give thanks to my God. Whenever I pray, I make my requests for all of you with joy, for you have been my partners in spreading the Good News about Christ from the time you first heard it until now. And I am certain that God, who began the good work within you, will continue his work until it is finally finished on the day when Christ Jesus returns.

A Kid's Story

Mark sat in the principal's office, nervously tapping his foot on the carpet.

"It's good to meet you face to face," the principal said. "I liked reading your application."

This made Mark feel more confident. "Thanks!" he said. "Being a principal's helper sounds like fun."

"What do you think will be fun about it?" the principal asked.

Oh no. José was stumped. He couldn't think of a good answer. He looked around the principal's office. His eyes rested on a poster of a surfer with the words "Be positive." José smiled.

"I guess it would be fun to come here in the morning and help with announcements. It would be fun to meet the other kids and get to know them. You know," José added, smiling at the surfer. "Most things at this school have been pretty fun. I think this would be another fun thing."

The principal smiled. "I love your positive attitude," he said. "Congratulations; you're hired."

The Bible Connects with Life

Joy and confidence are contagious—they make the people around you feel better. Paul's positive, confident attitude toward his friends, the Philippians, inspired them to be confident, too. Even though Paul wrote to them from prison, he mentioned the word joy sixteen times in one short letter. He started by saying that he prays with joy every time he thinks of the Philippians.

If you're not naturally joyful, do what Paul did. Remember the good things in your life, and thank God for them. You can be confident that God will give you a positive attitude because, as Paul writes, "I am certain that God, who began the good work within you, will continue his work until it is finally finished."

Joy and confidence are contagious—they make the people around you feel better.

Parents and Kids Try This Together

List three things you're grateful for right now, and then thank God for them. Do this out loud, taking turns with one another. If you have work that relates to any of these things, thank God for that, too. You can say something like, "Thank you, God, for my comfortable home. Thank you that I have time today to make it clean!"

Prayer

God, give me joy and confidence in you. May my positive attitude spread to the people around me. In Jesus' name, amen.

Day 25

You Can Be an Entrepreneur

Genesis 1:1; 27–28

In the beginning God created the heavens and the earth.

So God created human beings in his own image. In the image of God he created them; male and female he created them. Then God blessed them and said, "Be fruitful and multiply. Fill the earth and govern it. Reign over the fish in the sea, the birds in the sky, and all the animals that scurry along the ground."

A Kid's Story

Blake and his stepdad were raking leaves together when Blake asked, "Can I get paid for this?"

His stepdad looked surprised. "You want me to pay you for raking leaves?"

"I want to buy a soccer jersey, but Mom won't give me the money," Blake said.

"I see," his stepdad said. "Well, no one pays me to rake the leaves around here. But I'm glad you're interested in working for money. I wonder if there's something you can do that meets a need for someone else."

"What do you mean 'meets a need?'" Blake asked.

"People will only pay you money if you have something they need, like if they can't rake leaves themselves. When I was your age, I used to get two dollars a house for raking my neighbor's leaves."

"Two dollars? That'd take me forever to save up for a jersey! There's got to be something else I can do for money, something that people would pay me more for," Blake said.

"I see you've got the entrepreneurial spirit. You'll need to think up a product or service that meets someone's need more than raking leaves does."

"Hmm," Blake thought. "At my soccer games, parents look cold. They need something to warm them up. Maybe I could sell them hot cocoa!"

The Bible Connects with Life

Entrepreneurs are people who make it their job to start a new business. Entrepreneurs may come up with new ideas for products or services, or they might bring products or services to new places. The inventor of a phone app is an entrepreneur. So is someone who owns a food truck.

People are good at creating new things and spreading into new areas because that's how God designed people. God himself is creative. After all, he created everything, and God made people in his image. That means you're creative, too. You can't create the universe out of nothing, like God did. But you can create something new out of the materials God put in front of you.

Whether you create a product that makes money or a game that entertains your friends, you are being creative just like God. He created you that way.

You can create something new out of the materials God put in front of you.

Parents and Kids Try This Together

Brainstorm entrepreneurial ideas by focusing on the needs you see around you. Think of people you see most often. What do they need that they're not getting? Could you do something to meet those needs?

Prayer

God, thank you for making me creative. Help me see the needs of the people around me. In Jesus' name, amen.

Day 26

Create Job Opportunities

Jeremiah 29:4-7

This is what the LORD of Heaven's Armies, the God of Israel, says to all the captives he has exiled to Babylon from Jerusalem: "Build homes, and plan to stay. Plant gardens, and eat the food they produce. Marry and have children. Then find spouses for them so that you may have many grandchildren. Multiply! Do not dwindle away! And work for the peace and prosperity of the city where I sent you into exile. Pray to the LORD for it, for its welfare will determine your welfare."

A Kid's Story

Blake assembled the things he'd need for a hot cocoa stand: an insulated pitcher, cocoa mix, and paper cups. He put everything in his red wagon and stenciled in black letters: "Blake's Mobile Hot Cocoa."

That night at soccer, Blake got to work. He dragged his wagon down the sidelines, pouring cocoa and collecting money. The parents appreciated the hot drink and happily paid fifty cents per cup. At the end of the night, Blake had sold thirty cups of hot cocoa.

"I got fifteen dollars tonight!" Blake told his stepdad. "The cocoa and the cups cost me six dollars, so that means I made nine dollars profit."

"Way to go! What's next for Blake's Mobile Hot Cocoa?"

"Well, at this rate, it will still take me weeks to save up for that soccer jersey. Plus there are thirsty parents all over town."

"Could you do something to expand?" Blake's stepdad asked.

"That's it! I'll hire some neighborhood kids to work for me! They'll have fun, and we'll all make more money!"

The Bible Connects with Life

A good entrepreneurial idea benefits both you and the people around you. If you can meet a need in your city and people will pay for it, the next step is to hire others. Jeremiah 29:4–7 tells God's people to work for the prosperity of the city they're in. Starting a new business, meeting people's needs, and creating jobs are great ways to prosper your city.

Hiring workers is good for entrepreneurs because they can make more money from an expanded business. It's good for the workers because people flourish when they get to do productive work and make their own money. And if the product or service meets a genuine need, the whole city benefits.

Of course, not all new businesses succeed. Sometimes not enough people want the product, and it doesn't bring in enough money to buy supplies, pay workers, and make a profit. But some new businesses do succeed, and creating jobs is an important goal for entrepreneurs because citywide prosperity is God's goal.

Starting a new business, meeting people's needs, and creating jobs are great ways to prosper your city.

Parents and Kids Try This Together

Ask some friends to help you work on something that needs done in your city. If you can turn it into a business that makes money, even better!

Prayer

God, bless me with success so I can bless the people around me. I pray for the prosperity of my city. In Jesus' name, amen.

Day 27

Provide Opportunities

Leviticus 19:9–10

When you harvest the crops of your land, do not harvest the grain along the edges of your fields, and do not pick up what the harvesters drop. It is the same with your grape crop—do not strip every last bunch of grapes from the vines, and do not pick up the grapes that fall to the ground. Leave them for the poor and the foreigners living among you. I am the LORD your God.

A Kid's Story

After a week of "Blake's Mobile Hot Cocoa," Blake and his employees were selling hot cocoa all over town. Even the soccer players started buying drinks, and business boomed.

But Blake noticed one boy who never bought—he stood apart from the kids drinking cocoa.

"Want a drink?" Blake asked.

The boy looked at the ground and said, "I don't have any money."

Blake told his stepfather about it. "Some people don't have enough money for all the things they need or want," his stepfather explained.

"But that seems so unfair!"

"I agree."

"Should I give him a free cup of cocoa? He'd be happy, but the other kids would complain."

"I have an idea," his stepdad responded. Why don't you hire him? Then he can buy cocoa or anything else with the money you pay him."

"Hire him? But I don't know him at all," Blake said. "What if he drinks all the cocoa himself or doesn't give me the money he brings in?"

"Hmm. I guess that's the risk of hiring anybody. But entrepreneurs often take risks. Especially if it's the right thing to do."

The Bible Connects with Life

One of the best things a business can do is give jobs to people who can't otherwise support themselves. The Bible even has a law about this.

Leviticus 19:9–10 tells landowners to leave the edges of their fields unplowed so the poor and foreigners can harvest them. Any harvest that falls on the ground is free, too. This gave disadvantaged people productive work that brought them dignity, income, and future job skills.

It can feel uncomfortable to take a risk on someone who is different from you. Perhaps that's why God repeats over and over again this command to give work opportunities to the poor and foreigners. The rule also appears in Leviticus 23:22, Exodus 23:10–11, and Deuteronomy 24:19–22, which says,

When you are harvesting your crops and forget to bring in a bundle of grain from your field, don't go back to get it. Leave it for the foreigners, orphans, and widows. Then the LORD your God will bless you in all you do.

One of the best things a business can do is give jobs to people who can't otherwise support themselves.

Parents and Kids Try This Together

Is there a business in your city that hires people who wouldn't have jobs otherwise? Visit them, and ask how it's worked out. If you can't find one, try thinking of one that you would create yourself. What would it look like? Who would you hire? Why would you hire them?

Prayer

God, care for people who are poor and help me do your work in the world. In Jesus' name, amen.

Put God ahead of Money

Luke 12:16-21

"A rich man had a fertile farm that produced fine crops. He said to himself, 'What should I do? I don't have room for all my crops.' Then he said, 'I know! I'll tear down my barns and build bigger ones. Then I'll have room enough to store all my wheat and other goods. And I'll sit back and say to myself, "My friend, you have enough stored away for years to come. Now take it easy! Eat, drink, and be merry!"'

"But God said to him, 'You fool! You will die this very night. Then who will get everything you worked for?'

"Yes, a person is a fool to store up earthly wealth but not have a rich relationship with God."

A Kid's Story

Blake's new hire was working out well—so well that Blake didn't need to sell hot cocoa himself anymore. He oversaw his company's operations wearing the new jersey he'd bought with the profits, sipping from a custom thermos that read, "Blake's Mobile Hot Cocoa."

"What are you thinking about now?" his stepfather asked him.

"I just want to keep making money," Blake replied, "More and more."

"What do you want to use that money for?" his stepdad asked.

"I just want to keep it. I want to have the most money I can. Store up more and more. Then I'll never have to worry."

Blake's stepfather laughed. "I don't think it works that way."

"Why not?"

"Well, for one thing money, doesn't cure all worries. That's a God-sized job. And for another thing, it doesn't do you or your money any good when you hoard it or hide it under your mattress. You've got to get it moving. Invest it, or give it away."

The Bible Connects with Life

While the Bible encourages work and its rewards, there are many verses that warn against being too attached to your money. Jesus tells a story about a rich man who meets a nasty end because his reaction to success was to build bigger barns and save it all for himself. There's also Ecclesiastes 5:10, which says "those who love money will never have enough," and 1 Timothy 6:10, which calls the love of money "the root of all kinds of evil."

What should you do with your money other than store it? There are two good options: donate or invest.

Giving generously to people in need is a sign of faithfulness throughout the Bible. Plus it's a rule in 2 Corinthians 8:13–15. The other way to serve people with your money is to invest. Investing means loaning your money to someone else with the expectation of later getting it back with interest. Investment gives other people opportunities to start their own businesses, create jobs, and serve their communities with new products and services. Some investments specifically help poor people learn job skills and rise out of poverty.

Entrepreneurs honor God by making new things, creating jobs, and investing and donating money. Don't dishonor God by loving money more than him.

> Don't dishonor God by loving money more than him.

Parents and Kids Try This Together

Find an organization that does work you can invest in. Talk about how much you would like to invest and how you can start investing.

Prayer

God, thank you for investing in me. Please give me both success and compassion. In Jesus' name, amen.

Super Incredible Faith series for Girls and Boys

Help your children better understand how much God takes care of them! In these 100 devotions, Michelle Howe encourages kids to develop character traits including unconditional love, the fruits of the Spirit, the blessedness of the Beatitudes, and more. Each reflection includes a story, a Scripture verse, a prayer, and an activity page. **Ages 6 to 9.**

320 pages, Paperback, Full Color Illustrations

| Living Bravely | L50020 | ISBN: 9781628627800 |
| Conquering Fear | L50021 | ISBN: 9781628627824 |

Guided Journals for Girls and Boys

Preteen boys and girls will love these daily devotional journals that really encourage them to dig into the Bible. **Ages 10–12.**

136–160 pages, Paperback, Illustrated

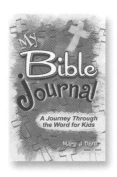 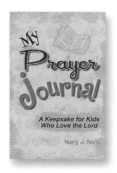

| My Bible Journal | L46911 | ISBN: 9781885358707 |
| My Prayer Journal | D46731 | ISBN: 9781885358370 |

Find more great stuff by visiting our website: **www.hendricksonrose.com**